FOR WALKERS & CYCLISTS

by Leslie Stanbridge

*A sixty-six mile route from
York Minster to Whitby Abbey, visiting many of the
most interesting pilgrimage sites in Yorkshire*

All profits from the sale of this book go to the charity Christian Aid
Published by Maxiprint, Kettlestring Lane, Clifton Moor, York YO30 4XF
printed@maxiprint.co.uk
January, 2000

THE ARCHBISHOP OF YORK

Preface
by the Archbishop of York, Dr David Hope

Over many years, many miles and in many countries, Leslie Stanbridge has honed his navigational skills to the very finest edge of excellence. He knows exactly what the walker – whether tyro or seasoned veteran – wants in a walking guide. More than that, in every sense himself a pilgrim, he knows, too, what it is that will enlighten and inspire a sense of pilgrimage in others. So it is then in 'The Whitby Way' Leslie offers, in the very fullest sense, a real *vade mecum*.

Detailed, accurate, informative and, above all, clear, it may be truly described as 'user-friendly'. More than that, however, it is also a positive joy! With its fine illustrations and its interesting and informative features on places and people encountered along the way, it affords almost as much pleasure as a fireside read as it does when consulted 'on the hoof'.

Almost, but not quite: for armchair pilgrimage is but a poor substitute for the real thing. So, put on the boots, pick up the book – and go for it! In our glorious North Yorkshire countryside and close to our Christian roots, you will not be disappointed.

+David Ebor:

Contents

Preface	2
About the Whitby Way	4
The Whitby Way in seven days	5
Along the Way	7
Symbols to diagrams	14
York Minster to the ring road	15
York ring road to the Jacobean Lodge	16
The Whitby Way by cycle	**17-20**
Jacobean Lodge to Huby	21
Huby to Crayke	22
Crayke to Oulston	23
Oulston to Byland	24
Byland to Ashberry Farm	25
Ashberry Farm to Helmsley	26
Helmsley to Howldale Lane	27
Beadlam to Kirkdale	28
Kirkbymoorside to Hutton-le-Hole	29
Lastingham to Rosedale Chimney	30
Rosedale Chimney to the ironstone kilns	31
Ironstone railway to Glaisdale Rigg	32
Fryup Head to East Arncliffe Wood	33
Along the Esk Valley	34
A bridle road to Sleights	35
Sleights to Whitby	36

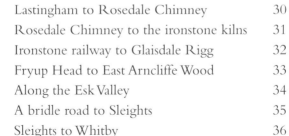

Futher copies of this book are available by sending a cheque for £5.25 *(this includes 75p for p&p)* made payable to 'Christian Aid', to: **Whitby Way, 171 Burton Stone Lane, York YO30 6DG**

About the Whitby Way

IT IS sixty-six miles from York to Whitby by the Whitby Way – but that is not the shortest route. Starting at York Minster and finishing at Whitby Abbey, it is designed to include some of the most interesting pilgrimage places in Yorkshire.

It can, of course, be enjoyed simply as a walk, for it goes through beautiful scenery. From the flat Vale of York it climbs to gently undulating country at Crayke. It crosses the North York Moors from south to north using field paths, moorland tracks and ancient paved ways. Finally, it follows the lush Esk Valley down to Whitby.

Someone said that a tourist passes through a place, but the place passes through a pilgrim. To walk the Whitby Way as a pilgrim is an invitation to leave time to be quiet, at Crayke and at Byland, at Rievaulx and Lastingham, at Kirkdale and Egton Bridge and, of course, in the cliff-top abbey ruins at Whitby which is the end of the way – at the top of the 199 steps!

The way starts at **York Minster,** scene of the re-birth of Christianity when in 627 King Edwin of Northumbria became a Christian and with him members of the royal family, including Hilda, soon to be abbess of the monastery at **Whitby.** But the statue of Constantine outside the Minster is a reminder that there were Christians in York when the Romans were there.

From Whitby, monks came to **Lastingham,** where the two saintly brothers, Cedd and Chad, were abbots, and the unforgettable Norman crypt of the present church, built not long after the Norman conquest, is still a focus of pilgrimage. Then there is **Crayke,** where St Cuthbert probably founded a monastery, and where his body rested for four months during the time the monks

from Lindisfarne were fleeing from the Viking invaders. **St Gregory's Minster** in Kirkdale also dates back to the time before the Normans.

The years of the twelfth century saw the great cathedrals built or re-built, and countless villages got new parish churches. Monasteries grew up all over the country, including those of the Cistercian monks, who sought out lonely places. The Whitby Way visits two of the finest Cistercian ruins at **Byland** and **Rievaulx.** The Benedictine abbey on the cliff top at **Whitby** was built not long after. In **Rosedale,** too, there was a small nunnery, and the present church is built where its choir stood.

After the Reformation came a time of great religious change, but some, particularly in lonely and remote areas like the North York Moors, clung to the old ways. But even there, the persecutors apprehended Nicholas Postgate, who became one of the last of the Catholic martyrs, hung, drawn and quartered in York in the final years of the seventeenth century. He is remembered in the Roman Catholic church at **Egton Bridge.**

Laurence Sterne, the eighteenth century novelist, would probably have been horrified to be included in a pilgrimage journey, but readers of his bizarre novel, *Tristram Shandy,* will be glad of the opportunity to visit the church at **Coxwold,** where he ministered, and to see Shandy Hall, where he lived.

Pilgrimage is not just looking back. It helps us to rediscover our own roots, and to re-equip ourselves for the everyday pilgrimage of life. Besides the obvious pilgrimage places, other churches on the Whitby Way, at Helmsley and Pockley, Kirkbymoorside and Glaisdale will be found open and welcoming to walkers and pilgrims with time to stop and rest.

The Whitby Way in Seven Days

Day 1 York to Huby *(10 miles)*
Start the day by visiting York Minster. Then walk across the flat country of the Vale of York to Huby. Overnight there or *(by bus)* in Easingwold or York.

Day 2 Huby to Coxwold *(9 miles)*
Walk to Crayke and visit the church; continue to Coxwold to see the church and beautiful village where Laurence Sterne was vicar. Overnight in Coxwold, Oldstead *(one mile off the route)* or Kilburn *(two miles off the route)*.

Day 3 Coxwold to Helmsley *(11 miles)*
Visit the abbey at Byland *(English Heritage)* and follow the ancient monks' road to Rievaulx *(English Heritage)*. Visit the abbey and continue to Helmsley for overnight.

Day 4 Helmsley to Kirkbymoorside *(8 miles)* or **Hutton-le-Hole** *(11 miles)*
Follow field paths via Pockley and Beadlam to St Gregory's Minster in Kirkdale. Continue to Kirkbymoorside or to Hutton-le-Hole for overnight.

Day 5 Kirkbymoorside *or* **Hutton-le-Hole to Rosedale Abbey** *(9 or 6 miles)*
An easy day with time to explore Lastingham and to cross the moor to Rosedale. Overnight in Rosedale.

Day 6 Rosedale Abbey to Glaisdale *(9 miles)*
Over the moor to Fryup Head and a long downhill stretch to the Esk Valley. Overnight in Glaisdale.

Day 7 Glaisdale to Whitby *(11 miles)*
Down the Esk Valley, visiting Egton Bridge, to Sleights and Whitby, finishing up the 199 steps to St Mary's Church and the abbey ruins.

Public transport

Huntington and Wigginton to York – a regular service of buses *(Rider York)*.

Huby, Crayke and Easingwold to York – served by the Reliance bus service *(01904 768262)*.

Coxwold, Wass and Helmsley – occasional buses operated by Stephensons *(01347 838990)*.

Helmsley to Kirkbymoorside and Scarborough – an hourly service operated by Scarborough and District Motor Services *(01723 375463)*. Links at Pickering and Thornton Dale with the Yorkshire Coastliner service *(see below)*.

Hutton-le-Hole and Rosedale – served by the Moorsbus on Sundays and some weekdays from May to September *(details from tourist information centres)*.

Glaisdale, Egton Bridge, Grosmont, Sleights and Whitby – an infrequent train service on the Esk Valley line, connecting at Middlesbrough with trains to the main line north and south. There are occasional buses from Egton Bridge to Whitby and a regular service from Sleights.

Whitby to Leeds, via York. The Yorkshire Coastliner service *(01653 692556)*.

Accommodation

Overnight accommodation is plentiful in York, Helmsley and Whitby, and there are youth hostels in all three places.

There is abundant bed and breakfast accommodation in the Esk Valley *(Glaisdale to Sleights)* and also in the southern part of the North York Moors. Accommodation is relatively scarce in villages south of the moors, but a list published by the Easingwold tourist information centre, Chapel Lane, Easingwold YO61 3AE includes addresses in Huby and Sutton on Forest *(one mile off the Whitby Way)*, Crayke and Coxwold, as well as Easingwold, Kilburn and Oldstead *(three miles, two miles and one mile off the route)*.

The following tourist information centres operate a local bed and breakfast service for the same night, and can supply lists of addresses:

York★	01904 620557
Easingwold	01347 821530
Helmsley	01439 770173
Malton	01653 600048
Pickering★	01751 473791
Danby	01287 660654
Scarborough★	01723 373333
Whitby★	01947 602674

★open all the year round

Maps

The diagrams in this book are intended to be used in conjunction with Ordnance Survey maps.

Landranger (1:50,000)	105	York and surrounding area
	100	Malton, Pickering and surrounding area
	94	Whitby
Pathfinder (1:25,000)	664	York *(west)*
	665	York *(east)* *From York to the Jacobean Lodge Hotel*
	654	Tollerton *From the Jacobean Lodge Hotel to just south of Crayke*
	642	Dalton and Coxwold *From just south of Crayke to Byland*

| Outdoor Leisure (1:25,000) | North York Moors *(26/27)* *From just north of Coxwold to Whitby* |

For the Whitby Way by cycle – Landranger (1:50,000) sheets 94, 100 and 105, as above and also Scarborough (sheet 101).

Facilities

	transport - bus/train	bed & breakfast	pub food	shop(s)	telephone	tourist information	bank	public toilet
York	○	○	○	○	○	○	○	○
Wigginton/Haxby	○		○	○				
Huby	○	○	○	○				
Crayke		○	○		○			
Coxwold		○	○	○	○			○
Byland/Wass		○		○	○			○
Rievaulx		○			○			○
Helmsley	○	○	○	○	○	○	○	○
Pockley					○			
Beadlam/Nawton	○	○	○	○				
Kirkbymoorside	○	○	○	○			○	○
Hutton-le-Hole		○	○		○			○
Lastingham		○	○		○			
Rosedale		○	○	○	○			○
Glaisdale	○	○	○		○			○
Egton Bridge	○	○			○			○
Grosmont (1 mile off route)	○	○	○	○	○			○
Sleights	○	○	○		○			
Ruswarp	○	○		○	○			○
Whitby	○	○	○	○	○	○	○	○

Along the Way

York Minster

YORK MINSTER has two claims to fame: it is the largest Gothic church north of the Alps, and it has more ancient glass than any other church in England. But the pilgrim will make for the crypt. That is the place to recall the year 627, when King Edwin of Northumbria accepted baptism. The beautiful font cover shows pictures of Edwin; his Christian queen, Ethelburga; Paulinus, her chaplain, who baptized Edwin; Hilda, who became Abbess of Whitby and was christened at the same time; and James the Deacon who assisted Paulinus. Edwin, Paulinus and Hilda are also pictured behind the three altars. The site of the first cathedral built by Edwin is unknown. The present minster was started in 1080, after the Norman Conquest, but the Norman church was completely transformed during the four hundred years which followed. The present minster was finished in 1472.

Pilgrims to York in the Middle Ages did not come to remember Edwin and Paulinus. There was a shrine behind the high altar to St William of York, who, after waiting for fourteen years until a pope was willing to recognise him as archbishop, died (or was murdered) shortly after returning to the city in 1154. He was recognised as a saint in 1223, and his shrine is now in the western crypt, where the great pillars of the second Norman choir, built around 1170, still stand. The crypt is open from 9:30am on weekdays and 1:30pm on Sundays.

Free leaflets about things to see in the minster are on the stands at the back of the nave, and a pilgrimage leaflet is available from the information desk, incorporating pilgrim prayers on a walk-round tour of the minster. Outside the south transept are two reminders of Roman York, where there were already Christians in the early fourth century. Across the road is a pillar from the Roman basilica, and close to the Minster is a splendid bronze statue of Constantine, who was proclaimed Emperor in York in 306.

From York to Huby

FROM the south transept of the minster, the Whitby Way leads along Goodramgate, named after the Viking Guthrun who was in York in 929, and through fourteenth-century Monk Bar to the River Foss at Monk Bridge. Here a leper hospital stood during the Middle Ages, at the northern extremity of the city. Beyond was the wild and dangerous Forest of Galtres, stretching north for over ten miles. Stripped of woodland in the seventeenth century, there is little wild about the area now.

The Whitby Way follows the **River Foss** for three miles to Huntington church. In the late eighteenth century the river was transformed into a canal to provide navigation up to Sheriff Hutton, but by 1845 the upper reaches were silted up, and navigation was abandoned beyond the city boundary. The remains of the locks can be seen from the riverside path.

Huntington church is in a rural setting, but serves a very large suburban area. Only the south doorway and the chancel remain from the medieval church. The busy York ring road is crossed safely by an underpass and footpaths lead to **Wigginton** pond. The village church nearby dates only from 1860, though there was an earlier building, and the village existed as a clearing in the forest before the Norman conquest.

From Wigginton the way leads across flat country on an old drovers' road, partly unmade, passing 'Bohemia' – the name dates from the seventeenth century – and reaching **Huby**. The 'by' in the village name reveals its Viking origins as a suburb of the Anglo-Saxon settlement of Sutton-on-the-Forest, a mile to the east, where the parish church stands. Laurence Sterne ministered here before moving to Coxwold.

Huby has a good shop and a fish and chip shop, and there is a motel. A two hourly bus service links the village with York and Easingwold.

Crayke and St Cuthbert

CRAYKE occupies a wonderful hilltop site, 379 feet above sea level, looking over the flat Vale of York. The name of the inn, the Durham Ox, is a reminder of St Cuthbert. The village still formed part of County Durham until the early nineteenth century, and the Dean and Chapter of Durham still appoint the Rectors of Crayke.

Cuthbert was born around 634, a native of the southern upland country of Scotland. He became a monk at Old Melrose in 651. The monastery nestled in the Tweed valley below the hill now known as Scott's view. Cuthbert became renowned as a fearless missionary among the wild people of the hills and as a great man of prayer and discipline. From Melrose he was called to the monastery at Lindisfarne to teach and train the monks. Often he sought solitude on the little St Cuthbert's Island off the shore near the church on Holy Island. Later he built a cell on the remote Inner Farne Island, where a chapel remains to his memory. Very reluctantly he agreed to become Bishop of Lindisfarne, and was consecrated in York Minster, and it was then in 685 that he was given Crayke, the first halting place on the ancient road north from York. He built a monastery on the hilltop, though its site is unknown.

Cuthbert's tomb on Holy Island was venerated by pilgrims until the Vikings invaded. The monks then fled with the coffin, attempted but failed to escape to Ireland, and then travelled from place to place. In the year 882 or 883 they were received by Geve, the Abbot of Crec, and stayed four months 'as if they had been in their own home.' Then they moved on to Chester-le-Street and eventually to Durham, where the wooden remains of Cuthbert's coffin and his pectoral cross can be seen in the Cathedral treasury. Pilgrims visit the shrine behind the high altar and use the prayer printed below.

Nothing remains in Crayke Church of the early monastery, for the present building dates from the fifteenth century. It possesses two pulpits, for preaching and for reading the service, and bobbin-headed pews, from the seventeenth century, and an earlier screen. Behind the church is Crayke Castle, now a country house, but originally built by the bishops of Durham. It was dismantled in the

Civil War in 1647, but part of the structure is medieval.

Although the village has not been improved by inappropriate modern development, there are attractive cottages and houses around the village green. The more easterly alternative route to Coxwold passes Crayke Manor, an early seventeenth century house.

Open our eyes, Lord, to see your glory;
Open our ears, Lord, to hear your call;
Open our lips, Lord, to sing your praises.

Then guide us on our pilgrimage of faith,
that with the memory of Cuthbert
in our minds,
and the spirit of Cuthbert in our hearts,
we may walk with him who is the Way, the
Truth and the Life, and find our
freedom in his service;
even our Lord and Saviour, Jesus Christ.

(A prayer used in Durham Cathedral)

From Coxwold to Rievaulx

OXWOLD was at one time a small market town, but long before the eighteenth century the market had vanished. Fine houses line the wide village street, including the old grammar school, founded in 1603, opposite the church; the early seventeenth century Colville Hall, just to the west of the churchyard; and a hospital for ten old men founded by Earl Fauconburg at the end of the seventeenth century. Outside the village, beyond the church, is Shandy Hall, the earliest part of which dates from the seventeenth century. It was lived in for seven years by Laurence Sterne, the novelist, before he died in 1768.

COXWOLD CHURCH has one of only two octagonal church towers in Yorkshire –

the other is at Sancton, in the East Riding. It was rebuilt in the fifteenth century, but retains excellent panels of medieval glass in the top lights of the nave windows. Excellent furniture of the seventeenth century includes a fine three-decker pulpit and a unique communion rail. The Fauconburg memorials to members of the Bellasis family, who lived at Newburgh Priory, a mile from the village, dominate the chancel.

Well-marked field paths lead from Coxwold to **BYLAND ABBEY,** one of the five finest Cistercian ruins in the north of England – the others are Rievaulx, Fountains, Furness and Kirkstall. It was founded in the mid-twelfth century by a group of monks from Furness Abbey. They did not find it easy to discover a site for their monastery, for they first settled too close to Rievaulx, at Old Byland, and then near Kilburn. Finally, they were given the land at Byland and built a magnificent church, 100 metres long and forty-three metres wide at the

transepts. The aisle walls stand to their full height, but only the west wall, with the remains of a glorious rose window, and the south transept, give any impression of the loftiness of the church, which was of a splendour far surpassing the austerity of the first Cistercian churches. Large areas of beautiful floor tiling remain, and there is quite a lot of the abbey buildings to see, including the cloister, which was one of the largest in the country. The Abbey is managed by English Heritage and is open during the summer months.

Crossing the main A170 road from Thirsk to Helmsley above Wass, the Whitby Way follows the ancient monk's road to **RIEVAULX.** The hollow road passes through pasture and alongside woodland to Ashberry Farm, in the valley of the river Rye. A loop northwards provides good winter views of Rievaulx Abbey, crosses the fine eighteenth century Bow Bridge, and then follows one of the medieval water channels that supplied the abbey. The village church at Rievaulx, restored in 1906, incorporates part of a small chapel which stood outside the monastery gate. The valley must have been thronged with people travelling to and from the great abbey, inhabited by 140 monks and 600 lay brothers. In the fifteenth and sixteenth century it was busy with iron mining.

Rievaulx and St Aelred

IEVAULX, like Byland, was a Cistercian monastery, founded in 1131 directly from Clairvaux, the mother house of the order in France, by St Bernard's own monks. It was under the patronage both of the king and of Thurstan, the Archbishop of York, and was regarded as the foremost abbey of the order in England. Its reputation grew still more through its saintly third abbot, Aelred, known as 'the Bernard of the north'.

Aelred was the son of a priest at Hexham. He was educated in Durham, and as a young man of twenty joined the household of David I, King of Scotland. The story is told of how he visited York on business, and then rode to Helmsley where Walter L'Espec, founder of Rievaulx, entertained him at his castle. He was taken to Rievaulx to see the abbey and meet the monks. He realised that this was to be his home. He entered the community, and in spite of his delicate health survived the austere regime. In 1143 he was made Abbot of Revesby, in Lincolnshire, and was called back to his own monastery to be abbot there from 1147 until his death in 1167.

He brought a gentle holiness to the community which did much to humanise the harshness of the Cistercian life, and the monastery attracted able people like himself. He was esteemed as a preacher and wrote lives of Edward the Confessor and of St Ninian. But he is best known for his treatise on friendship, which reflected his own character. 'In true friendship one travels by making progress,' he wrote, and the abbey under Aelred was a place where the friendship of Christ was valued and practised. And at the heart of friendship is love, the love of God who created us to share his love and to love one another.

Rievaulx is still a place of peace. Of the earlier church, built in the twelfth century in an austere style, parts remain in the nave and the transepts. But about 1230 the east end of the church was transformed by the building of the superb early Gothic choir, still impressive in its roofless state. Much remains of the community buildings, including the vast refectory. Rievaulx owes its preservation to the eighteenth century owner of the Duncombe estate, who created the terraces on the hill above the abbey as a platform from which to view the picturesque ruin. The terraces are managed by the National Trust and are open during the summer (entrance on the B1257 road). The abbey is managed by English Heritage and is open throughout the year.

From Helmsley to Hutton-le-Hole

HELMSLEY, with its large market place and picturesque houses, has a church built in the twelfth century, though much altered down the years. The south door and the chancel arch are from the earliest church. Behind the church is the 16th century Canons' Garth which probably belonged to the Augustinian canons of Kirkham Priory, near Malton. The castle (English Heritage: open throughout the year, closed from 1:00pm to 2:00pm) was built by Robert de Roos in the years following 1190, and part of the keep is of that date. It was restored by the parliament forces in the Civil War and was then dismantled. The mound provides a pleasant place to sit, high above the tourists crowding the town.

Following field-paths across Riccal Dale, known for its wild flowers, the Whitby Way reaches **Pockley.** This was one of the villages in the Duncombe Park estate. In the eighteenth century the farmers were 'a poor wretched sort of people' and it seems that the villages were left to decline. Consequently, in Pockley, as well as in Beadlam and Harome, there are single-storied, stone-walled, cruck-built thatched-roof longhouses, which originally comprised a parlour, a forehouse (that is, the main living room with a fireplace), the entrance passage, and, on the far side of it, the byre. They were probably built in the seventeenth century. West View is a good example, and so is White Cottage, though that has been extended.

The way skirts Beadlam and Nawton to reach Kirkdale and **St Gregory's Minster.** Although not an ancient place of pilgrimage, the church is now one of the most visited in the diocese. Founded probably in the early Anglo-Saxon period – the seventh century – as a minster church (that is, a church with a small community of priests ministering in the surrounding area), it was rebuilt by Orm, the son of Gamal, in the eleventh century.

The record of the rebuilding is on the stone above the south doorway, which has a pre-conquest sundial marked with the eight hours of the Anglo-Saxon day. The narrow arch in the tower is from the Saxon church; the arcade of the nave is twelfth century, and so is the font.

Kirkbymoorside, from 'time out of mind' a market town, boasted two castles in the middle ages, the Stuteville castle near the church, and a hunting box of the Nevilles, north of the town. The nave is the earliest part of the church, dating from the thirteenth century, and there is a fine medieval porch. The town is much less a tourist centre than its neighbours, Helmsley and Pickering. The Black Swan has an interesting porch dated 1634, and there are some fine Georgian houses.

Crossing the lower part of Farndale, the Whitby Way arrives at the tourist honey-pot of **Hutton–le–Hole,** with its shops, cafes and the very interesting Ryedale Folk Museum, which is well worth a visit.

Lastingham and St Cedd

ASTINGHAM crypt is unforgettable. Built in 1078 by the monks from Whitby, it is a perfect aisled church, with eastern apse, chancel, nave and side aisles. It was built over the spot where St Cedd was thought to be buried.

Cedd was the oldest of four brothers who were trained at the abbey on Lindisfarne to be priests and missionaries. After preaching the gospel in central England, Cedd was consecrated as Bishop of the East Saxons, with his base at Bradwell in Essex, where the church still stands. From there he returned with two of his brothers, Caelin and Cynabil, to establish the monastery at Lastingham, then a remote and wild place. This was in 654. He took part in the Synod of Whitby in 664, when it was decided that the customs of the Roman church rather than of the Celtic church should be the way forward for the

church in England, but shortly after his return to Lastingham he died of the plague. When a stone church was later built, his remains were re-buried near the altar.

Following Cedd's death, his brother Chad became abbot in his place, but he was first called away to take temporary charge of the diocese of York, and then was consecrated Bishop of Lichfield, where he is revered as a saint.

Nothing remains at Lastingham of the pre-conquest churches, except for some of the stones exhibited in the crypt and perhaps the foundation stones of the four Norman pillars. The monastery continued until the Viking invasions, and was re-founded in 1078 as a Benedictine community by monks from Whitby Abbey. They built the present church and crypt, but never finished the work, as they were invited to start St Mary's Abbey in York. The church has remained the parish church of the village, and was carefully restored at the end of the nineteenth century by the eminent architect, J L Pearson, who constructed the vaults in the upper church. In the village there are wells of St Cedd and St Chad.

From Lastingham to Glaisdale

ROM Lastingham, the Whitby Way climbs northwards across the moorland to **Ana Cross.** The crosses, of which there are many in the North York Moors, were probably erected as waymarks on the ancient paths, and Ana may have been the name of a real person. The track north from Lastingham was presumably used by the monks on their way to Whitby.

The road from Hutton-le-Hole to Rosedale is crossed at **Rosedale Chimney.** The actual

chimney, built for smelting iron ore, was demolished some years ago, but the name persists as a title for the steep road dropping into the valley. The kilns remain nearby.

A spectacular path descends to **Rosedale Abbey,** the village named after the small priory of Cistercian nuns founded in 1140. The present church, restored in 1894 and recently beautified, occupies the site of the choir of the nunnery church. Of the rest, only one stone pillar remains. The village grew during the development of ironstone working in the middle of the nineteenth century.

A fine section of the ironstone railway is followed from **Hill Cottages** northwards, with magnificent views of the upper dale. The kilns in which the ore was partly smelted are being preserved. After treatment, the ore was carried by rail round the heads of Rosedale and Farndale, and then winched down an incline to Battersby Junction, en route for Middlesbrough. Built in 1861, the railway was taken up in 1929. There was ironstone quarrying in Rosedale and in the Esk Valley long before the ore was extracted on a large scale.

The track leading from the railway across the moor to **Fryup Head** is one of a number of stone-flagged causeways in the area. Known as **George Gap causeway,** it was used by packhorses carrying salt, fish and iron. At Fryup Head there are remains of old coal mines.

The descent to the Esk Valley is by a broad moorland track – 'the Whitby road', as a wayside stone calls it – leading down **Glaisdale Rigg** to the village. Like Rosedale, **Glaisdale** grew in the nineteenth century from a scattered hamlet to a large village as a result of the mining and quarrying. The railway line through the Esk Valley was built in 1865, when iron mining was at its height. It still offers an infrequent but scenic journey to Whitby.

Beggars' Bridge, close to Glaisdale station, has existed since the fourteenth century, but was rebuilt in 1619 by Thomas Ferris, an alderman of Hull, as a help to wayfarers crossing the River Esk when it was in flood. Glaisdale is left by another old paved path through **Arncliffe Wood.**

From Glaisdale to Whitby

HE Roman Catholic church in **Egton Bridge,** dedicated to St Hedda, remembers Nicholas Postgate, a good and holy man, firm in the faith of his fathers. Born in the village before 1600, he was brought up in the old faith, for his grandfather was known as 'a recusant who teacheth children.' Nicholas was trained for the Roman Catholic priesthood and returned from the continent to a perilous ministry in England. Around 1663 he came back to the North York Moors to give pastoral care and  celebrate Mass for the scattered families who had not accepted the Reformation. In 1679 he was taken to York to be hung, drawn and quartered at the age of eighty, one of the last of the eighty-five martyrs honoured by the Pope in 1987.

A private road, which is a right of way for walkers and cyclists, leads to Grosmont. On the way an old toll house proclaims a list of charges in shillings and pence.

From the outskirts of Grosmont a bridle road passes the elegant **Newbiggin Hall,** built in the seventeenth century, and leads to the bridge at **Sleights.** Field-paths avoid the dangerous and busy road from Sleights to **Ruswarp,** and the final stages of the walk follow the old way into **Whitby.** There is a surprise last-minute view of the harbour.

Across the river, Church Street and the 199 steps climb to the parish church of St Mary and the abbey ruins. The steps date back to 1317, but were originally made of wood, replaced in stone in the eighteenth century. **St Mary's Church** is a mad mixture of medieval and Georgian, and is not to be missed. There is nothing like it anywhere else. The Norman chancel arch is obscured by the Cholmley family pew with its barley-sugar columns. Box pews fill every part of the church, except the ancient chancel, and the 1778 pulpit towers high above them.

Others may come to Whitby for Captain Cook or even for Dracula, but the pilgrim presses on to the abbey.

Whitby Abbey and St Hilda

WHITBY ABBEY was founded by St Hilda in 657. She was a member of the Northumbrian royal family and was baptised by Paulinus with King Edwin, in 627. 'A most devoted servant of Christ,' she entered the monastic life and became Abbess of Hartlepool. There she taught the virtues of justice, devotion and chastity, and above all, the way of living together in peace and charity. No one was rich, and no one in need, for the nuns held all things in common.

On the same principles she founded the double monastery of nuns and monks on the cliff top at Whitby in 657. Soon its reputation was widely known, and it was chosen as the scene of the Synod of Whitby, which in 664 decided the future of the English church. Hilda's abbey became a school for bishops, and it was at Whitby under Hilda that Caedmon discovered that he was marked out by the grace of God to compose religious songs and poems in his own tongue. Hilda died in 680, and a line of distinguished abbesses followed her. The Viking invasions in 867 brought the community to an end. Bede speaks of lofty buildings, but only one building of considerable size has been discovered, though excavations have revealed a number of small cells and evidence of spinning and weaving.

The abbey was re-founded after the Norman Conquest by Benedictine monks from Evesham and Winchcombe. Parts of the early church are marked out in the turf, but the present choir was not begun until 1220, the transepts and the east part of the nave in 1260 and the west part of the church not until fourteenth century. By then the church was 300 feet long.

The monastery was suppressed in 1538, but the church survived intact until 1711. The Nave collapsed later in the eighteenth century and the tower in the nineteenth. The desolation was not improved by direct hits from a German cruiser in 1914. Very little remains of the abbey buildings, apart from the church, since the stone was used for the seventeenth century Abbey House, home of the Cholmley family, who bought the site after the monastery was dissolved.

The abbey is managed by English Heritage, which publishes a useful and well-illustrated guide. It is open throughout the year.

· · · · · · · ·

Now we must praise the ruler of heaven,
The might of the Lord and his purpose of
mind,
The work of the Glorious Father; for he
God Eternal, established each wonder,
He, Holy Creator, first fashioned the heavens
As a roof for the children of earth.
And then our Guardian, the Everlasting Lord,
Adorned this middle-earth for men.
Praise the Almighty King of Heaven.

Caedmon

THE COUNTRY CODE
- Enjoy the countryside and respect its life and work
- Guard against all risk of fire
- Fasten all gates
- Keep to public paths across the farm land
- Leave livestock, crops and machinery alone
- Use gates and styles to cross fences, hedges and walls
- Take your litter home
- Help to keep all water clean
- Protect wildlife, plants and trees
- Take special care on country roads
- Make no unnecessary noise.

Route diagrams

Symbols on diagrams

The main route `- - - -`

Alternative route `·· ... ··...`

Hedges/fences `··· -·-.`

Mileages from York and Whitby – **15/51**

The red letters (**A, B,** etc) refer to the notes

Signpost –	**SP**
Footpath sign –	**FP**
Bridle road sign –	**BR**
Stile –	**S**
Gate –	**G**
Telephone –	**T**
Footbridge –	**FB**
Public house –	**PH**

Every effort has been made to achieve total accuracy but no responsibility can be accepted for errors or omissions by the publishers, nor any consequence arising from the use of the information.

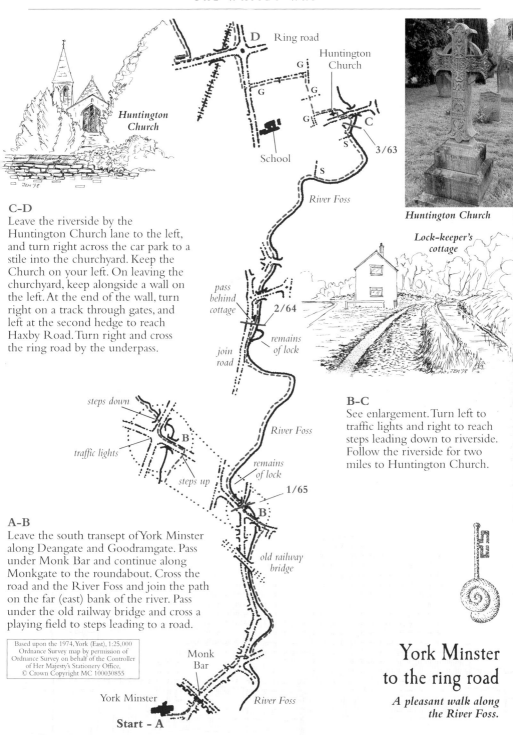

Huntington Church

D Ring road

Huntington Church

G

G G

G

School

C

3/63

S

S

River Foss

Huntington Church

C-D
Leave the riverside by the Huntington Church lane to the left, and turn right across the car park to a stile into the churchyard. Keep the Church on your left. On leaving the churchyard, keep alongside a wall on the left. At the end of the wall, turn right on a track through gates, and left at the second hedge to reach Haxby Road. Turn right and cross the ring road by the underpass.

Lock-keeper's cottage

pass behind cottage

2/64

join road

remains of lock

steps down

River Foss

B-C
See enlargement. Turn left to traffic lights and right to reach steps leading down to riverside. Follow the riverside for two miles to Huntington Church.

B

traffic lights

steps up

remains of lock

1/65

B

A-B
Leave the south transept of York Minster along Deangate and Goodramgate. Pass under Monk Bar and continue along Monkgate to the roundabout. Cross the road and the River Foss and join the path on the far (east) bank of the river. Pass under the old railway bridge and cross a playing field to steps leading to a road.

old railway bridge

Monk Bar

York Minster

River Foss

Start - A

York Minster to the ring road

A pleasant walk along the River Foss.

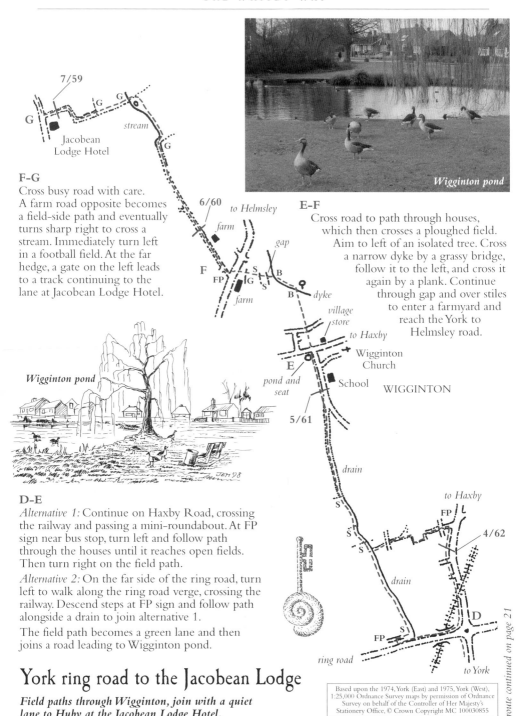

Wigginton pond

7/59

G   G
G
stream
Jacobean
Lodge Hotel

F-G
Cross busy road with care.
A farm road opposite becomes
a field-side path and eventually
turns sharp right to cross a
stream. Immediately turn left
in a football field. At the far
hedge, a gate on the left leads
to a track continuing to the
lane at Jacobean Lodge Hotel.

6/60
to Helmsley
farm
gap
F
FP   S   B
G   S
S   B   dyke
farm

E-F
Cross road to path through houses,
which then crosses a ploughed field.
Aim to left of an isolated tree. Cross
a narrow dyke by a grassy bridge,
follow it to the left, and cross it
again by a plank. Continue
through gap and over stiles
to enter a farmyard and
reach the York to
Helmsley road.

village
store
to Haxby

Wigginton
Church

E
pond and
seat

School

WIGGINTON

5/61

drain

Wigginton pond

JEH 98

D-E
Alternative 1: Continue on Haxby Road, crossing
the railway and passing a mini-roundabout. At FP
sign near bus stop, turn left and follow path
through the houses until it reaches open fields.
Then turn right on the field path.

Alternative 2: On the far side of the ring road, turn
left to walk along the ring road verge, crossing the
railway. Descend steps at FP sign and follow path
alongside a drain to join alternative 1.

The field path becomes a green lane and then
joins a road leading to Wigginton pond.

to Haxby
S   FP   L
S
4/62
S
drain
D
FP   S
ring road
to York

York ring road to the Jacobean Lodge

*Field paths through Wigginton, join with a quiet
lane to Huby at the Jacobean Lodge Hotel.*

Based upon the 1974, York (East) and 1975, York (West),
1:25,000 Ordnance Survey maps by permission of Ordnance
Survey on behalf of the Controller of Her Majesty's
Stationery Office, © Crown Copyright MC 100030855

route continued on page 21

16

The Whitby Way by Cycle – a five-day tour

Day 1 – (33 miles)

Leave York by the riverside cycle path to **Skelton.** Cross the A19 and pass through the village, following a quiet lane (partly unmade) to **Huby.** Continue across the Easingwold-Stillington road to **Crayke.**

Follow quiet roads through **Oulston** to **Coxwold.** Turn right to follow signed cycle route to **Byland Abbey,** and then left through **Oldstead** to a junction of cycle routes. Here turn right and climb to the A170. Turn right towards **Helmsley** and then left for a downhill run through **Scawton** to **Rievaulx.** Join B1257 for overnight at **Helmsley.**

Day 2 – (34 miles)

Avoid the fast A170 by following lanes through **Harome,** Wombleton and **Welburn.** Cross the A170 to Kirkdale (**St Gregory's Minster**) and continue to **Kirkbymoorside.** Either (a) follow a lane to Ravenswick, cross the footbridge and climb on an unmade road to join the main Hutton-le-Hole road; or (b) take the A170 for a short distance towards Scarborough, turn left through Keldholme and join the Hutton-le-Hole road. At **Hutton-le-Hole,** turn right for **Lastingham.**

Continue through Lower Askew to join the main Rosedale road. Turn left to reach **Hartoft.** Beyond the Inn, turn right and then left to climb steadily to the Rosedale-Egton Bridge road. Follow this

Rievaulx Abbey

across Egton High Moor and drop steeply *(1 in 4)* to **Egton Bridge.**

An unmade private road opposite the church leads to **Grosmont.** At the top of the main street, turn left for **Sleights.** Drop through the village on the A169 and cross the bridge over the River Esk. Immediately, turn right for **Ruswarp.** Turn right over the river at Ruswarp, and left into Larpool Lane, which winds to the A171. Turn left towards **Whitby** and right to climb to the abbey and youth hostel.

Day 3 – (20 miles)

Return to Larpool Lane and pick up the railway path southwards through **Robin Hood's Bay** and **Ravenscar** to Scalby. Turn left to reach the A165 and the youth hostel.

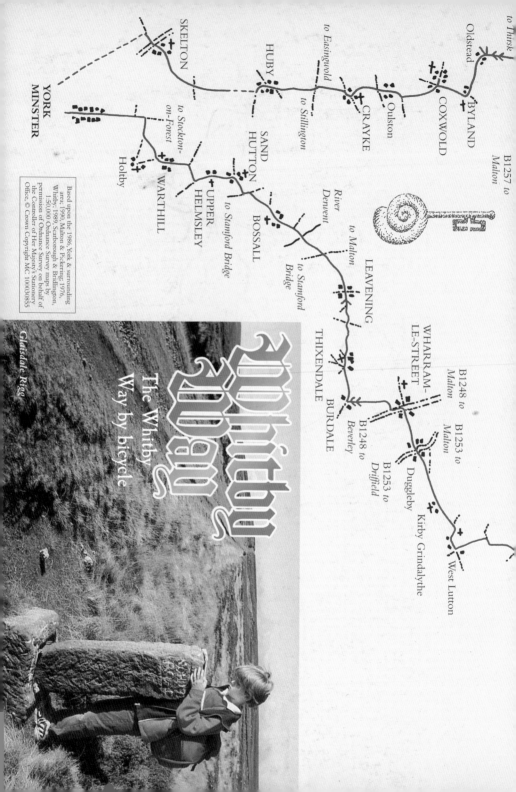

Whitby Way

The Whitby Way by bicycle

YORK MINSTER

SKELTON

HUBY

to Easingwold

to Stillington

OULSTON

CRAYKE

COXWOLD

BYLAND

Oldstead

to Thirsk

B1257 to Malton

to Stockton-on-Forest

Holtby

WARTHILL

UPPER HELMSLEY

SAND HUTTON

BOSSALL

to Stamford Bridge

River Derwent

to Stamford Bridge

to Malton

LEAVENING

THIXENDALE

BURDALE

WHARRAM-LE-STREET

B1248 to Malton

B1253 to Malton

B1248 to Beverley

B1253 to Driffield

Duggleby

Kirby Grindalythe

West Lutton

Glaisdale Rigg

Based upon the 1986, York & surrounding area, 1990, Malton & Pickering, 1976, Whitby, 1989, Scarborough & Bridlington, 1:50,000 Ordnance Survey maps by permission of Ordnance Survey maps on behalf of the Controller of Her Majesty's Stationery Office. © Crown Copyright MC 100030855

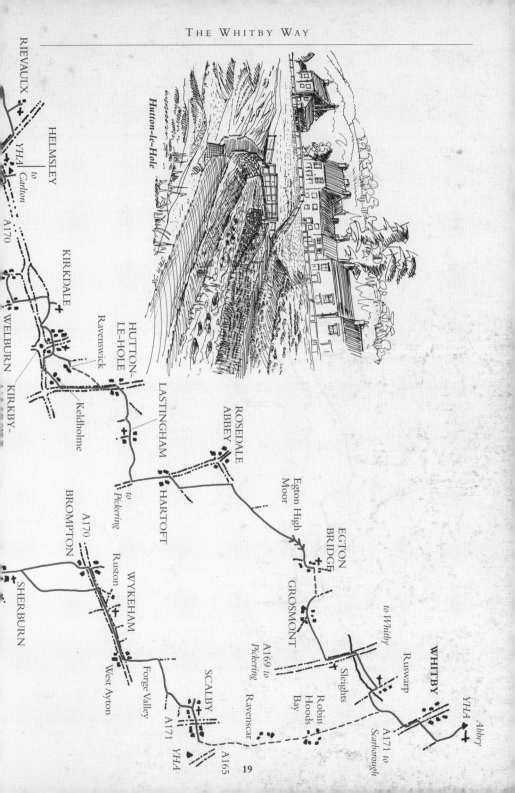

RIEVAULX

HELMSLEY

YHA to Carlton

A170

KIRKDALE

WELBURN

KIRKBY-

Ravenswick

Keldholme

HUTTON-LE-HOLE

Hutton-le-Hole

LASTINGHAM

to Pickering

ROSEDALE ABBEY

HARTOFT

BROMPTON

A170

Ruston

WYKEHAM

West Ayton

SHERBURN

Forge Valley

Egton High Moor

EGTON BRIDGE

GROSMONT

A169 to Pickering

Sleights

Robin Hoods Bay

to Whitby

Ruswarp

WHITBY

YHA

Abbey

A171 to Scarborough

to Ravenscar

SCALBY

A171

A165

YHA

19

Day 4 – (31 miles)

Pass through **Scalby** village to reach Lady Edith's Drive and **Forge Valley.** At **West Ayton** turn right along A170 either (a) to Ruston. Turn left towards Sherburn; or (b) to **Brompton:** see village and church (where Wordsworth was married) and continue to **Sherburn.**

Cross A64 at Sherburn traffic lights and fork right for **West Lutton.** Turn right, passing Kirby Grindalythe and Duggleby to **Wharram-le-Street** (church tower built before the Norman conquest). Follow B1248 towards Malton for a short distance and then turn right, dropping steeply into Burdale. Turn right for **Thixendale.**

Day 5 – (21 miles)

From Thixendale, climb to Leavening Brow and drop steeply into **Leavening.** Continue to **Howsham Bridge** over the River Derwent, and fork left to **Bossall.** See the fine church and continue, forking left and then right for **Sand Hutton.** Turn left in village for **Upper Helmsley** and in a further $1/2$ mile, right and then left for **Warthill.** Beyond the church, take minor road on right to join the Holtby-Stockton road. Turn right, and then second left into Stockton Lane, to reach York Minster.

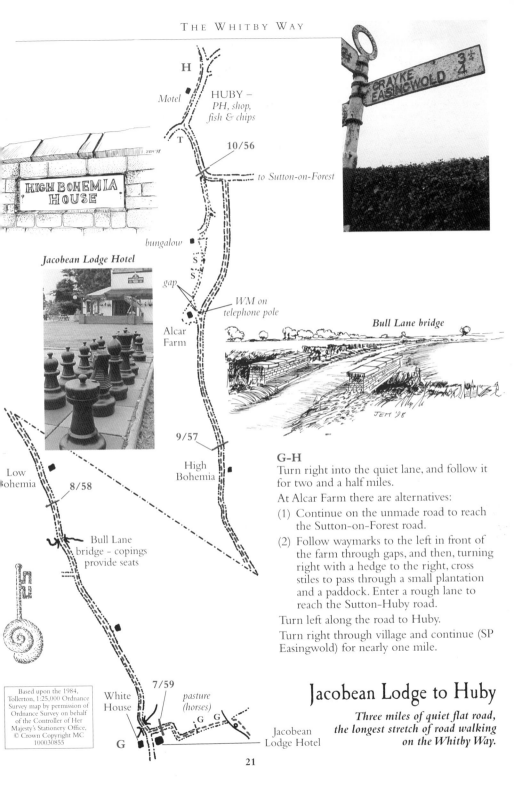

H

Motel

HUBY –
*PH, shop,
fish & chips*

HIGH BOHEMIA HOUSE

T

10/56

to Sutton-on-Forest

bungalow

Jacobean Lodge Hotel

S

gap

S

*WM on
telephone pole*

Alcar
Farm

Bull Lane bridge

9/57

High
Bohemia

G-H

Turn right into the quiet lane, and follow it
for two and a half miles.

At Alcar Farm there are alternatives:

(1) Continue on the unmade road to reach
the Sutton-on-Forest road.

(2) Follow waymarks to the left in front of
the farm through gaps, and then, turning
right with a hedge to the right, cross
stiles to pass through a small plantation
and a paddock. Enter a rough lane to
reach the Sutton-Huby road.

Low
Bohemia

8/58

Bull Lane
bridge - copings
provide seats

Turn left along the road to Huby.

Turn right through village and continue (SP
Easingwold) for nearly one mile.

7/59

White
House

*pasture
(horses)*

G G

G

Jacobean
Lodge Hotel

Jacobean Lodge to Huby

*Three miles of quiet flat road,
the longest stretch of road walking
on the Whitby Way.*

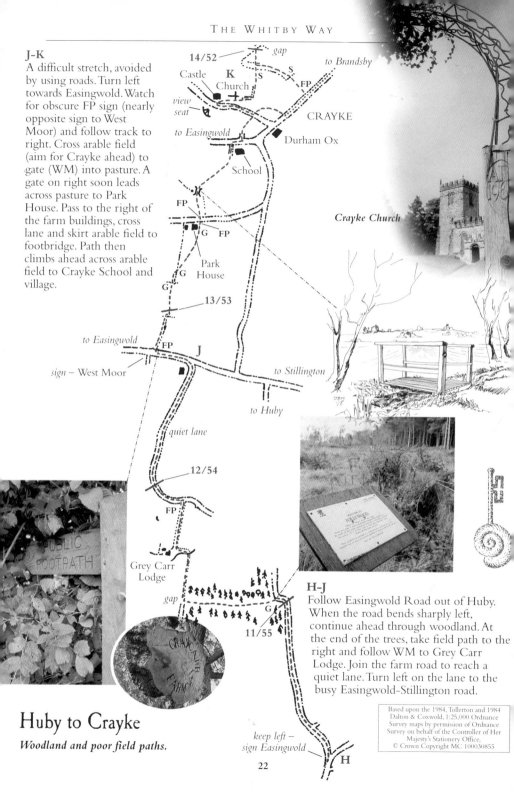

J-K
A difficult stretch, avoided by using roads. Turn left towards Easingwold. Watch for obscure FP sign (nearly opposite sign to West Moor) and follow track to right. Cross arable field (aim for Crayke ahead) to gate (WM) into pasture. A gate on right soon leads across pasture to Park House. Pass to the right of the farm buildings, cross lane and skirt arable field to footbridge. Path then climbs ahead across arable field to Crayke School and village.

14/52
gap
to Brandsby
Castle K
Church S
FP
view seat
CRAYKE
to Easingwold
Durham Ox
School

Crayke Church

FP
G FP
Park House
G
G
13/53

to Easingwold
FP
J
to Stillington
sign – West Moor
to Huby

quiet lane

12/54
FP

PUBLIC FOOTPATH

Grey Carr Lodge
gap
G
11/55

CRAYKE CARR FARM

H-J
Follow Easingwold Road out of Huby. When the road bends sharply left, continue ahead through woodland. At the end of the trees, take field path to the right and follow WM to Grey Carr Lodge. Join the farm road to reach a quiet lane. Turn left on the lane to the busy Easingwold-Stillington road.

Huby to Crayke

Woodland and poor field paths.

keep left – sign Easingwold
H

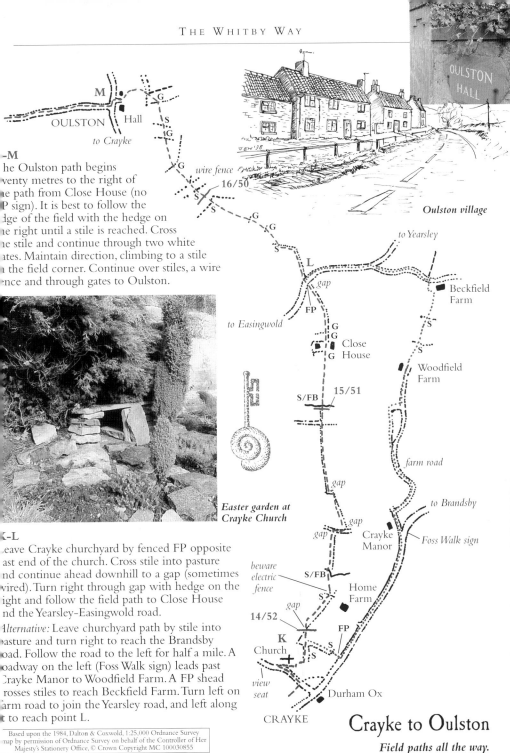

OULSTON HALL

Oulston village

Easter garden at Crayke Church

M
OULSTON Hall
G
S
G
to Crayke

G *wire fence*
16/50
S
S G
G
S

to Yearsley

L
gap
FP
Beckfield
Farm

to Easingwold
G
G
Close
G House

S

S

Woodfield
Farm

S/FB 15/51

farm road

gap

to Brandsby

gap
gap Crayke Foss Walk sign
Manor

beware
electric S/FB
fence Home
S Farm
gap

14/52 FP
K S
Church S

view
seat Durham Ox

CRAYKE

–M

he Oulston path begins
venty metres to the right of
ιe path from Close House (no
P sign). It is best to follow the
dge of the field with the hedge on
ιe right until a stile is reached. Cross
ιe stile and continue through two white
ates. Maintain direction, climbing to a stile
ι the field corner. Continue over stiles, a wire
·nce and through gates to Oulston.

¬-L

eave Crayke churchyard by fenced FP opposite
ast end of the church. Cross stile into pasture
nd continue ahead downhill to a gap (sometimes
vired). Turn right through gap with hedge on the
ight and follow the field path to Close House
nd the Yearsley-Easingwold road.

Alternative: Leave churchyard path by stile into
·asture and turn right to reach the Brandsby
oad. Follow the road to the left for half a mile. A
oadway on the left (Foss Walk sign) leads past
⁻rayke Manor to Woodfield Farm. A FP ¬head
rosses stiles to reach Beckfield Farm. Turn left on
¬arm road to join the Yearsley road, and left along
¬t to reach point L.

Crayke to Oulston

Field paths all the way.

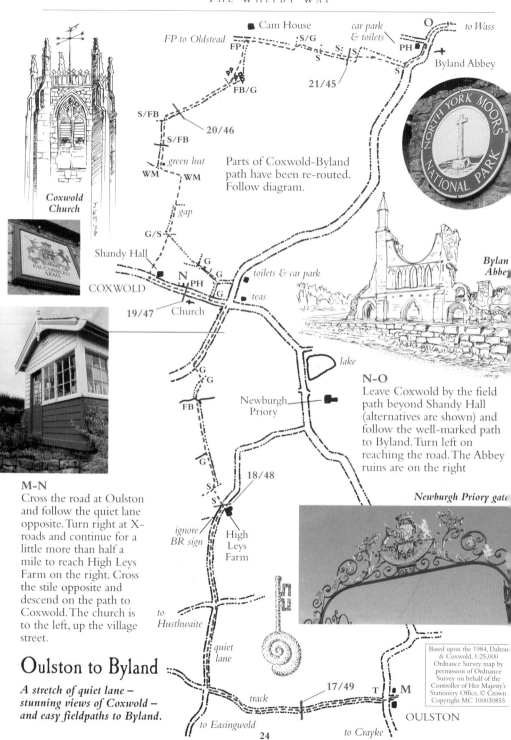

Cam House

FP to Oldstead

car park & toilets

O

to Wass

S/G

FP

S:

S:

PH

+

21/45

S

Byland Abbey

FB/G

S/FB

20/46

S/FB

green hut

WM   WM

Parts of Coxwold-Byland path have been re-routed. Follow diagram.

Coxwold Church

JE7 '08

gap

G/S

Shandy Hall

G

G

toilets & car park

COXWOLD

N

PH

G

teas

Bylan Abbe

19/47   Church

G
G

lake

FB

Newburgh Priory

N-O
Leave Coxwold by the field path beyond Shandy Hall (alternatives are shown) and follow the well-marked path to Byland. Turn left on reaching the road. The Abbey ruins are on the right

G

18/48

M-N
Cross the road at Oulston and follow the quiet lane opposite. Turn right at X-roads and continue for a little more than half a mile to reach High Leys Farm on the right. Cross the stile opposite and descend on the path to Coxwold. The church is to the left, up the village street.

S
S

ignore BR sign

High Leys Farm

Newburgh Priory gate

to Husthwaite

quiet lane

Oulston to Byland

A stretch of quiet lane – stunning views of Coxwold – and easy fieldpaths to Byland.

17/49   T   M

track

OULSTON

to Easingwold

to Crayke

Based upon the 1984, Dalton & Coxwold, 1:25,000 Ordnance Survey map by permission of Ordnance Survey on behalf of the Controller of Her Majesty's Stationery Office, © Crown Copyright MC 100030855

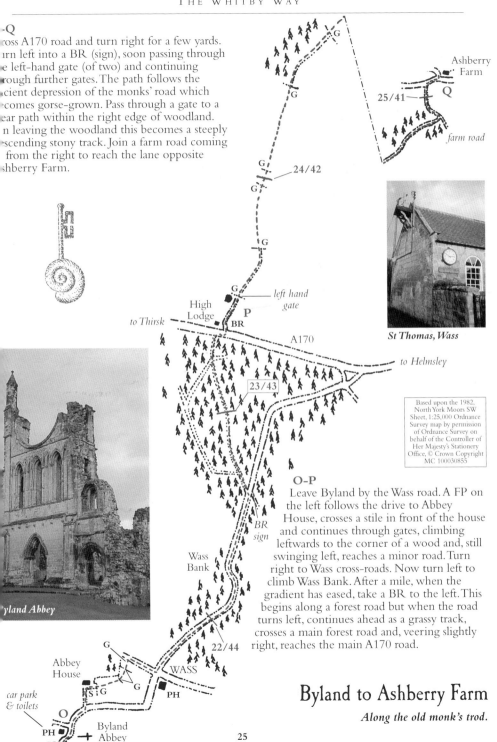

-Q
oss A170 road and turn right for a few yards.
rn left into a BR (sign), soon passing through
e left-hand gate (of two) and continuing
rough further gates. The path follows the
cient depression of the monks' road which
comes gorse-grown. Pass through a gate to a
ear path within the right edge of woodland.
n leaving the woodland this becomes a steeply
scending stony track. Join a farm road coming
from the right to reach the lane opposite
hberry Farm.

Ashberry
Farm

25/41

Q

farm road

24/42

St Thomas, Wass

High
Lodge
to Thirsk
BR
P
left hand
gate
A170
to Helmsley

23/43

Based upon the 1982,
North York Moors SW
Sheet, 1:25,000 Ordnance
Survey map by permission
of Ordnance Survey on
behalf of the Controller of
Her Majesty's Stationery
Office, © Crown Copyright
MC 100030855

O-P
Leave Byland by the Wass road. A FP on
the left follows the drive to Abbey
House, crosses a stile in front of the house
and continues through gates, climbing
leftwards to the corner of a wood and, still
swinging left, reaches a minor road. Turn
right to Wass cross-roads. Now turn left to
climb Wass Bank. After a mile, when the
gradient has eased, take a BR to the left. This
begins along a forest road but when the road
turns left, continues ahead as a grassy track,
crosses a main forest road and, veering slightly
right, reaches the main A170 road.

BR
sign
Wass
Bank

yland Abbey

22/44

Abbey
House
WASS
car park
& toilets
S G
G
PH
O
PH
Byland
Abbey
to Coxwold

25

Byland to Ashberry Farm
Along the old monk's trod.

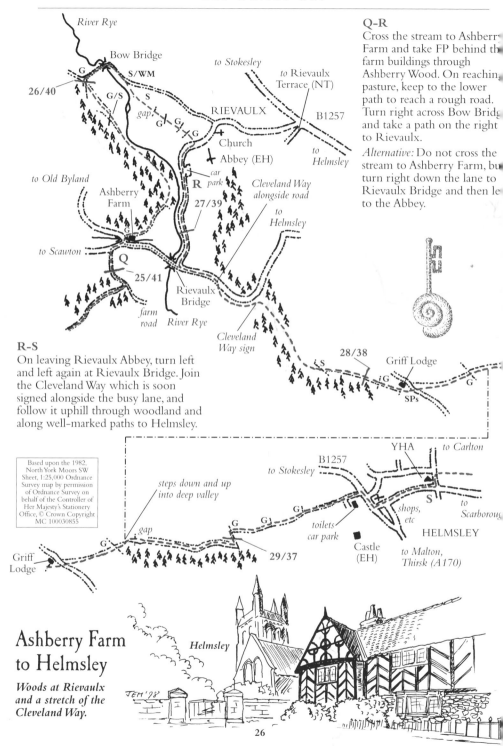

Q-R

Cross the stream to Ashberry Farm and take FP behind the farm buildings through Ashberry Wood. On reaching pasture, keep to the lower path to reach a rough road. Turn right across Bow Bridge and take a path on the right to Rievaulx.

Alternative: Do not cross the stream to Ashberry Farm, but turn right down the lane to Rievaulx Bridge and then left to the Abbey.

R-S

On leaving Rievaulx Abbey, turn left and left again at Rievaulx Bridge. Join the Cleveland Way which is soon signed alongside the busy lane, and follow it uphill through woodland and along well-marked paths to Helmsley.

Based upon the 1982, North York Moors SW Sheet, 1:25,000 Ordnance Survey map by permission of Ordnance Survey on behalf of the Controller of Her Majesty's Stationery Office, © Crown Copyright MC 100030855

Ashberry Farm to Helmsley

Woods at Rievaulx and a stretch of the Cleveland Way.

JEH '98

-V

the third thatched cottage on the right (Daleside), a
turns right to join a track from the church and
ephone box. Turn right on this track through gates and
en left, following field edge (hedge on left) to a short
iced section. Cross a grassy valley and climb through
e trees opposite. Emerge from the trees to turn right
d then left on field sides to the north-west corner of
arr Wood. Turn right alongside the wood, and then left
cross minor road and reach sunken Howldale Lane.

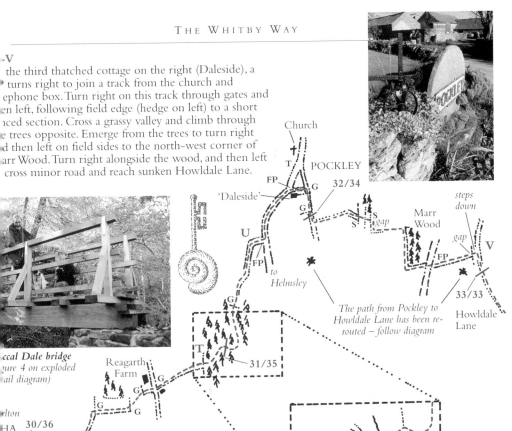

Church

POCKLEY

32/34

'Daleside'

U

Marr
Wood

gap

steps
down

gap

V

FP

to
Helmsley

33/33

The path from Pockley to
Howldale Lane has been re-
routed – follow diagram

Howldale
Lane

ccal Dale bridge
ure 4 on exploded
ail diagram)

Reagarth
Farm

31/35

lton
HA 30/36

to Scarborough

HELMSLEY

Based upon the 1982, North York Moors
SW Sheet, 1:25,000 Ordnance Survey map
by permission of Ordnance Survey on
behalf of the Controller of Her Majesty's
Stationery Office, © Crown Copyright
MC 100030855

-T

om Helmsley Square, follow the Scarborough
ad, and then turn left (sign: Carlton). FP starts
n the right in a few yards (opposite YHA).
ollow through gates and along field side and
en turn right over pasture, climbing past the
orner of a wood (on the left), and on to
eagarth Farm. Across the farm road, a path
ads to the edge of wooded Riccal Dale.

T-U

Crossing of Riccal Dale (see enlargement). Enter
woodland. After thirty metres, fork right (1)
downhill to T-junction with a broad track. (2)
Turn left: ignore tempting path on right (after
thirty metres), and walk a further seventy metres
to find a very narrow path (3) – easy to miss –
dropping to a footbridge (4). Cross the bridge
and follow a narrow path across the valley floor,
ignoring side turnings and bearing slightly right
before swinging left (5) into a wooded side
valley. Leaving the woodland, the path soon
becomes a green lane. On reaching the Pockley
road, turn left towards the village.

Helmsley to Howldale Lane

Fieldpaths and a wilderness crossing of Riccal Dale.

ockley

27

W-X

Turn left on minor road and then right to follow the roadway and track past Lund Head. On reaching a minor road, turn right, and left at the next junction (sign: Hold Caldron). When the road reaches woodland, take BR right. In a few yards, fork right and then follow field edges to Kirkdale. The Minster is to the left.

Alternative: Continue on the road to Hold Coldran, cross the bridge and turn right down the valley to St Gregory's.

X-Y

Leave St Gregory's by the road towards Kirkbymoorside. At the first cross-roads, a FP enters pasture through a gate. Climb to a stile in the far right-hand corner of this field, and continue on well-used path to Kirkbymoorside

Hold
Caldron

BR

G

G

Lund
Head

34/32

W

gap

V

G

Howldale
Lane

Gx2

steps
down

G G

School

A170 to
Scarborough

A170 to
Helmsley

NAWTON

BEADLAM

sign Hold
Caldron

35/31

G

St Gregory's
Minster

G

to
Fadmoor

Y

S

to Ki
moors

36/30

G

G

X

to
Helmsley

KIRKDALE

ford/FB

St Gregory's Minster

V-W

Turn right down Howldale Lane. By the first bungalow on the left, take a fenced path which then crosses pasture to Nawton. Cross High Street and go forward along School Lane. Leave School Lane by FP opposite school, passing through two wicket gates and crossing a large pasture diagonally to the opposite corner. Follow WMs through gates to right-hand of cottages ahead and to a minor road.

Beadlam to Kirkdale

Fieldpaths to St Gregory's Minster.

Jen '9

Nawto

-Z
ontinue over stiles and then through houses to
irkbymoorside. Turn right down the main street.
ave the town by Howe End, at the lower end of
arket Place. When the road turns right, FP enters
recreation field and climbs ahead, following field
lges to a minor road. Turn left, and then right, past
avenswick to a footbridge over the River Dove.
he unmade road ahead leads to the main
utton-le-Hole road.

-A
ross with care, and use the
ide verge on right side of road
itil FP sign is reached. Follow
ith to the right and in a few
irds (sign) turn left steeply
own to a footbridge. Cross the
ridge, pass to the right of the
ees opposite and climb steeply
reach a gate on Oxclose
ane. Turn left to
utton-le-Hole.

iotograph by Leslie Stanbridge

A–B
The Lastingham
path leaves
opposite the
village hall and
crosses pasture
to the edge of
the moor and
the Lastingham
road.

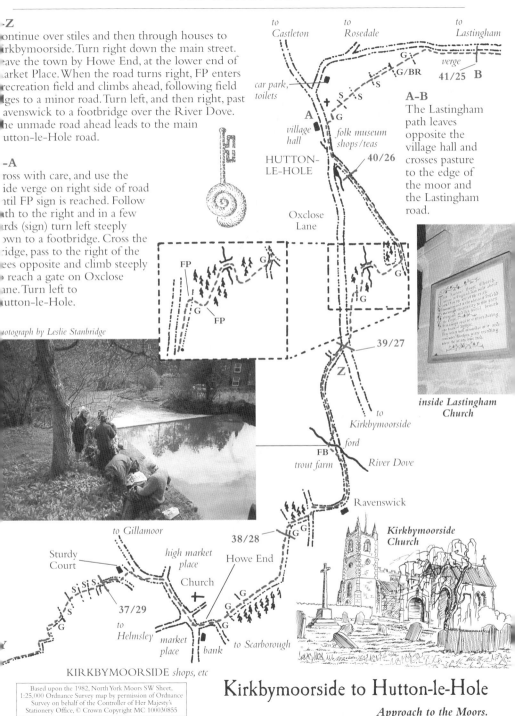

*inside Lastingham
Church*

*Kirkbymoorside
Church*

KIRKBYMOORSIDE *shops, etc*

Kirkbymoorside to Hutton-le-Hole

Approach to the Moors.

29

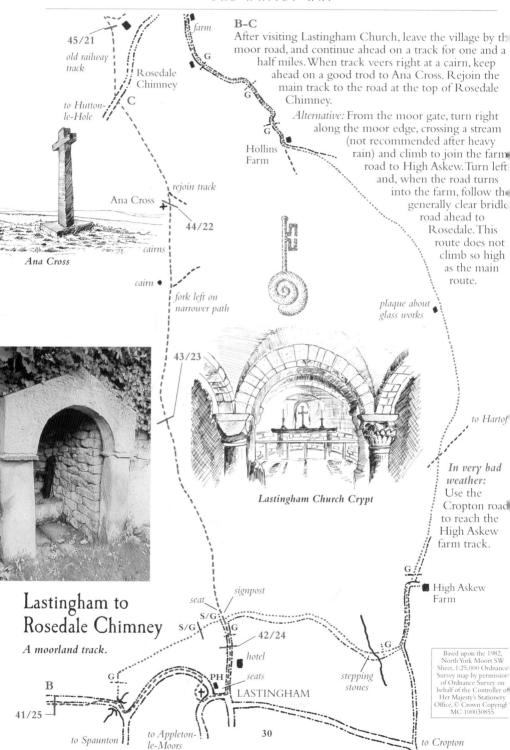

45/21
old railway track

farm

G

Rosedale Chimney

C

to Hutton-le-Hole

Ana Cross

rejoin track

Ana Cross
+
44/22

cairns

cairn •

fork left on narrower path

43/23

Lastingham Church Crypt

B-C

After visiting Lastingham Church, leave the village by the moor road, and continue ahead on a track for one and a half miles. When track veers right at a cairn, keep ahead on a good trod to Ana Cross. Rejoin the main track to the road at the top of Rosedale Chimney.

Alternative: From the moor gate, turn right along the moor edge, crossing a stream (not recommended after heavy rain) and climb to join the farm road to High Askew. Turn left and, when the road turns into the farm, follow the generally clear bridle road ahead to Rosedale. This route does not climb so high as the main route.

Hollins Farm

G

G

G

G

plaque about glass works

to Hartof

In very bad weather: Use the Cropton road to reach the High Askew farm track.

G

High Askew Farm

Lastingham to Rosedale Chimney

A moorland track.

seat

signpost

S/G

S/G   G

42/24

hotel

B

G

PH

seats

+

LASTINGHAM

stepping stones

to Spaunton

to Appleton-le-Moors

to Cropton

41/25

G

30

Based upon the 1982, North York Moors SW Sheet, 1:25,000 Ordnance Survey map by permission of Ordnance Survey on behalf of the Controller of Her Majesty's Stationery Office, © Crown Copyright MC 100030855

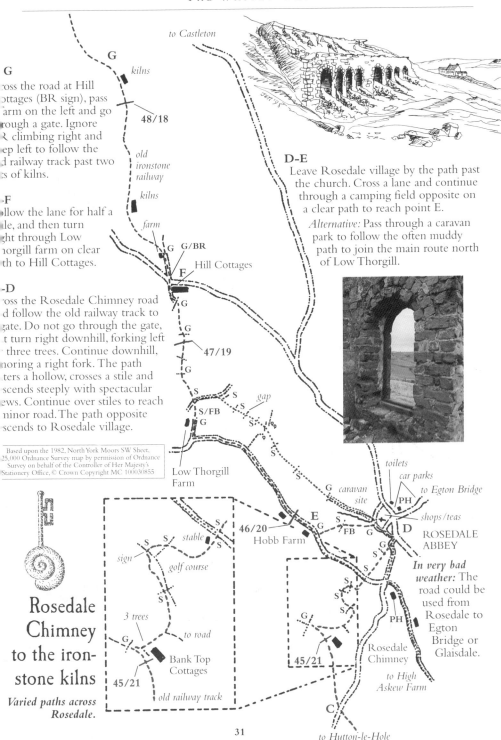

to Castleton

G

kilns

G
...oss the road at Hill
...ottages (BR sign), pass
...arm on the left and go
...rough a gate. Ignore
...R climbing right and
...ep left to follow the
...d railway track past two
...ts of kilns.

48/18

*old
ironstone
railway*

kilns

D-E
Leave Rosedale village by the path past
the church. Cross a lane and continue
through a camping field opposite on
a clear path to reach point E.

Alternative: Pass through a caravan
park to follow the often muddy
path to join the main route north
of Low Thorgill.

..F
...llow the lane for half a
...le, and then turn
...ght through Low
...horgill farm on clear
...th to Hill Cottages.

farm

G G/BR

Hill Cottages

F

..-D
...oss the Rosedale Chimney road
...d follow the old railway track to
...gate. Do not go through the gate,
...t turn right downhill, forking left
... three trees. Continue downhill,
...noring a right fork. The path
...ters a hollow, crosses a stile and
...scends steeply with spectacular
...ews. Continue over stiles to reach
...ninor road. The path opposite
...scends to Rosedale village.

G

G

47/19

G

S   S   *gap*

S/FB   S
G   S

Low Thorgill
Farm

toilets

car parks

S

G *caravan
site*   PH   *to Egton Bridge*

E   *shops/teas*

S   S   *stable*   S   46/20   G

sign   S   Hobb Farm   FB   G   D

golf course   S   G   **ROSEDALE
ABBEY**

S   *In very bad
weather:* The
road could be
used from
Rosedale to
Egton
Bridge or
Glaisdale.

Rosedale
Chimney
to the iron-
stone kilns

*Varied paths across
Rosedale.*

3 trees

S

G   *to road*

*Bank Top
Cottages*

45/21

old railway track

G

S

PH

*Rosedale
Chimney*

45/21

*to High
Askew Farm*

C

31

to Hutton-le-Hole

CARRY MAP AND COMPASS AND BE PREPARED TO USE THEM

G-H

Pass a ruined hut on left alongside railway. Shortly afterwards the track curves left on a high embankment. Cross the embankment and immediately turn right on a BR with the side valley on your right. BRs diverge – ignore a line of posts to the left – continue ahead, veering right to cross a small stream. Pick up a line of cairns and posts on an indistinct path to the Rosedale-Castleton road.

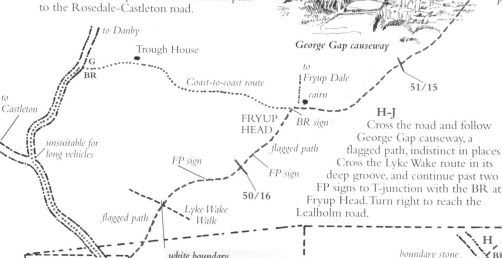

George Gap causeway

to Danby

Trough House

G
BR

Coast-to-coast route

to Castleton

unsuitable for long vehicles

FRYUP HEAD

to Fryup Dale

cairn

BR sign

51/15

flagged path

FP sign

FP sign

50/16

flagged path

Lyke Wake Walk

H-J

Cross the road and follow George Gap causeway, a flagged path, indistinct in places. Cross the Lyke Wake route in its deep groove, and continue past two FP signs to T-junction with the BR at Fryup Head. Turn right to reach the Lealholm road.

white boundary stone

BR ⊢ BR

H

49/17

high embankment

ruined hut

G

48/18

to Rosedale

H
B

boundary stone

follow posts BR

cairns *cross runnel*

prominent cairn

bridle roads diverge: ignore posts to left

cross stream

high embankment

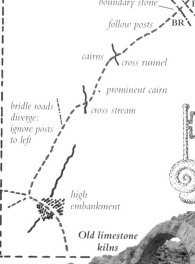

Old limestone kilns

Ironstone railway to Glaisdale Rigg

A moorland crossing.

32

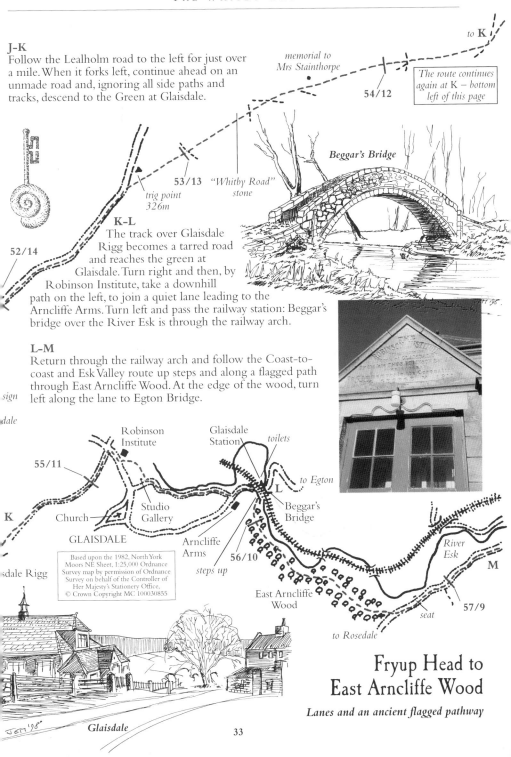

J-K
Follow the Lealholm road to the left for just over a mile. When it forks left, continue ahead on an unmade road and, ignoring all side paths and tracks, descend to the Green at Glaisdale.

memorial to Mrs Stainthorpe

54/12

to **K**

The route continues again at K – bottom left of this page

Beggar's Bridge

53/13 *"Whitby Road" stone*

trig point 326m

52/14

K-L
The track over Glaisdale Rigg becomes a tarred road and reaches the green at Glaisdale. Turn right and then, by Robinson Institute, take a downhill path on the left, to join a quiet lane leading to the Arncliffe Arms. Turn left and pass the railway station: Beggar's bridge over the River Esk is through the railway arch.

L-M
Return through the railway arch and follow the Coast-to-coast and Esk Valley route up steps and along a flagged path through East Arncliffe Wood. At the edge of the wood, turn *sign* left along the lane to Egton Bridge.

dale

Robinson Institute

Glaisdale Station

toilets

55/11

to Egton

L

K

Church

Studio Gallery

Beggar's Bridge

GLAISDALE

Arncliffe Arms

56/10

steps up

River Esk

M

dale Rigg

Based upon the 1982, North York Moors NE Sheet, 1:25,000 Ordnance Survey map by permission of Ordnance Survey on behalf of the Controller of Her Majesty's Stationery Office, © Crown Copyright MC 100030855

East Arncliffe Wood

seat

57/9

to Rosedale

Fryup Head to East Arncliffe Wood

Lanes and an ancient flagged pathway

Glaisdale

L-M

To cross the river Esk by the stepping stones, (not recommended when the river is in spate), watch for FP on the left opposite a road junction. Join the main route by the Roman Catholic Church (remember Nicholas Postgate). Follow the private road to Grosmont on the right just before the church. On reaching the Egton-Grosmont road, turn left for a few yards and then right on a bridleway (at first a narrow tarred lane), passing two farms.

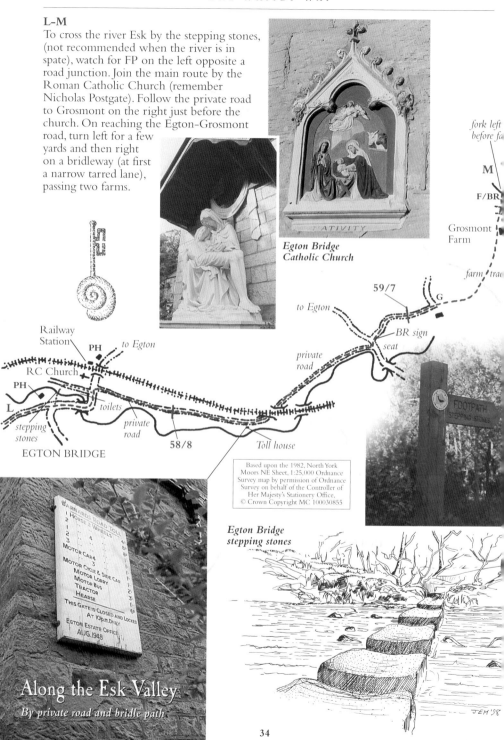

Egton Bridge
Catholic Church

fork left
before fa

M

F/BR

Grosmont
Farm

farm trac

59/7

to Egton

to Egton

Railway
Station

PH

RC Church

PH

L

stepping
stones

EGTON BRIDGE

toilets

private
road

private
road

58/8

BR sign

seat

Toll house

G

FOOTPATH
STEPPING STONES

Based upon the 1982, North York Moors NE Sheet, 1:25,000 Ordnance Survey map by permission of Ordnance Survey on behalf of the Controller of Her Majesty's Stationery Office, © Crown Copyright MC 100030855

Egton Bridge
stepping stones

Along the Esk Valley
By private road and bridle path

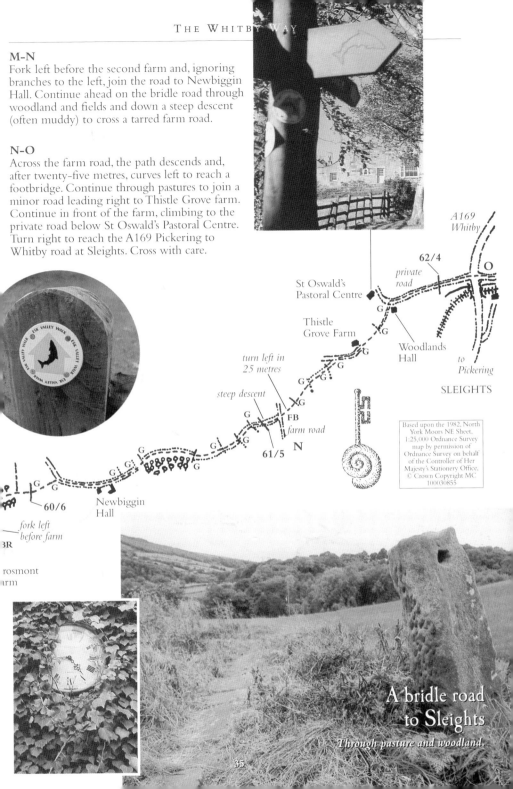

M–N

Fork left before the second farm and, ignoring branches to the left, join the road to Newbiggin Hall. Continue ahead on the bridle road through woodland and fields and down a steep descent (often muddy) to cross a tarred farm road.

N–O

Across the farm road, the path descends and, after twenty-five metres, curves left to reach a footbridge. Continue through pastures to join a minor road leading right to Thistle Grove farm. Continue in front of the farm, climbing to the private road below St Oswald's Pastoral Centre. Turn right to reach the A169 Pickering to Whitby road at Sleights. Cross with care.

A169
Whitby

62/4

private
road

O

St Oswald's
Pastoral Centre

G

Thistle
Grove Farm

G

Woodlands
Hall

to
Pickering

turn left in
25 metres

G

SLEIGHTS

steep descent

G

G

FB
farm road

61/5

N

60/6

Newbiggin
Hall

fork left
before farm

3R

rosmont
arm

A bridle road to Sleights
Through pasture and woodland.

35

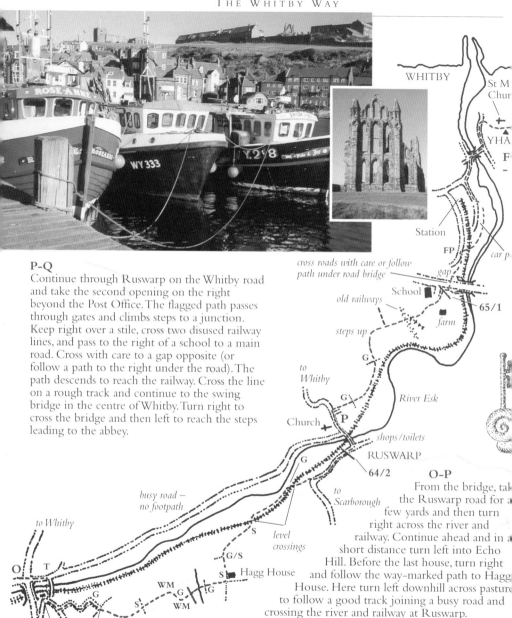

P-Q

Continue through Ruswarp on the Whitby road and take the second opening on the right beyond the Post Office. The flagged path passes through gates and climbs steps to a junction. Keep right over a stile, cross two disused railway lines, and pass to the right of a school to a main road. Cross with care to a gap opposite (or follow a path to the right under the road). The path descends to reach the railway. Cross the line on a rough track and continue to the swing bridge in the centre of Whitby. Turn right to cross the bridge and then left to reach the steps leading to the abbey.

WHITBY
St M
Chur
YHA
F
Station
FP · car p
cross roads with care or follow path under road bridge · gap
School
old railways · 65/1
farm
steps up
G
to Whitby
G
River Esk
Church · P
shops/toilets
G
RUSWARP
64/2
to Scarborough

O-P

From the bridge, take the Ruswarp road for a few yards and then turn right across the river and railway. Continue ahead and in a short distance turn left into Echo Hill. Before the last house, turn right and follow the way-marked path to Hagg House. Here turn left downhill across pasture to follow a good track joining a busy road and crossing the river and railway at Ruswarp.

busy road – no footpath
to Whitby
S
level crossings
O T
G/S
S
Hagg House
WM
G G G
S
WM
Station G/FP
SLEIGHTS
to Pickering A169

Based upon the 1982, North York Moors NE Sheet, 1:25,000 Ordnance Survey map by permission of Ordnance Survey on behalf of the Controller of Her Majesty's Stationery Office, © Crown Copyright MC 100030855

Sleights to Whitby

Field paths follow the River Esk.